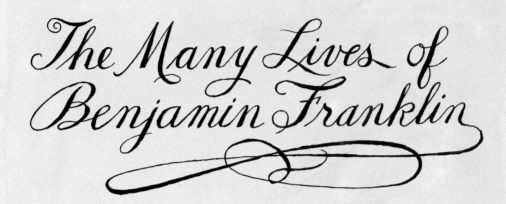

The Many Lives of Benjamin Franklin

Written down and illustrated by

Aliki

Prentice-Hall Inc.
Englewood Cliffs, N.J.

Prentice-Hall International, Inc., London
Prentice-Hall of Australia, Pty. Ltd., North Sydney
Prentice-Hall of Canada, Ltd., Toronto
10 9 8 7 6 5 4 3 2 1

Prentice-Hall of India Private Ltd., New Delhi
Prentice-Hall of Japan, Inc., Tokyo
Prentice-Hall of Southeast Asia Pte. Ltd., Singapore

Library of Congress Cataloging in Publication Data
Aliki. The many lives of Benjamin Franklin.
    SUMMARY: A simple biography of Benjamin Franklin emphasizing his contributions to American literature, politics, and science.
    1. Franklin, Benjamin, 1706-1790—Juvenile literature. 2. Statesmen—United States—Biography—Juvenile literature. [1. Franklin, Benjamin, 1706-1790. 2. Statesmen] I. Title.
E302.6.F8A48   973.3'092'4 [B] [92]   77-5508
ISBN 0-13-556019-5

The author wishes to thank John L. Roeder and Patricia Walker for their kind help.

for Carolyn W. Field

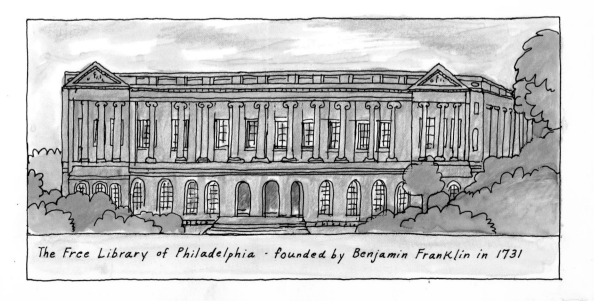

The Free Library of Philadelphia · founded by Benjamin Franklin in 1731

These are some of the 17 children of Josiah and Abiah Franklin. Ben was the tenth and youngest son.

'Tis a good thing the table is big.

JOSIAH FRANKLIN SOAP AND CANDLEMAKER

You can do this work when you grow up.

I don't like the smell.

Ben taught himself to read before anyone even noticed.

The house on Milk Street where Ben was born.

In 1706 in Boston, Benjamin Franklin was born with just one life. From the beginning, he was full of brilliant ideas and humor. As he grew, he put them to use. So he became a man with many lives.

Ben was the son of a candlemaker. His parents had many children but they saw Ben was special. He was curious. He loved books.

He had lots of his own ideas. Even at play, Ben was thinking.

He liked to swim, and often tried different ways. Once he made paddles so he could go faster.

Ben's paddles were wooden, with a hole for his thumb. He made paddles for his feet, too.

Another time he was kite flying near a pond and had a brighter idea. He went for a swim holding onto the kite string. Just as he had hoped, the kite pulled him across the pond.

Ben felt like taking a swim.

He tied his kite to a branch.

Then he had an idea.

He let the kite pull him across the pond, and his friend carried his clothes to the other side.

Ben started school, but his parents did not have the money for him to continue. After two years, the boy had to leave and choose a trade.

When he was 12, Ben was sent to live with his brother James. James was a printer. Ben would learn to be a printer, too.

Ben's job as an apprentice was to clean and sort type, sweep the floor, and sell newspapers.

THE
New-England Courant

Ben spent nights and Sundays reading and practicing his writing.

Ben learned quickly. He worked long hours. Still he found time to read every book he could borrow. He saved the money he earned to buy more.

At the shop, Ben wanted to do more than help print his brother's newspaper. He wanted to write in it! So he thought of a way.

James began finding letters under the office door. They were signed Silence Dogood. She wrote such clever essays, stories and poetry, James printed them. In fact they helped him sell more newspapers. Little did anyone know that Silence Dogood was Ben.

Silence Dogood wrote that she was a poor widow with some ideas she wished to share.

She said she would write again.

James showed the letters to his friends.

I don't know who she is, but I'll print them.

clever

interesting

funny

another letter!

People could hardly wait for Widow Dogood's next letter.

Ben wrote more and more letters.

But when James found out, he was angry. Ben was not allowed to write any more.

He decided to go somewhere else, where he could write. So when he was 17, he left James and Boston.

Ben went to Philadelphia to start a life of his own. He found a job with a printer. He read and collected more books. He worked and saved until at last he bought his own shop. Now he could print his own newspaper and all the letters he wished.

Philadelphia 1723

Ben worked very hard and even delivered his packages himself.

When Ben was 24, he married Deborah Read. Deborah worked hard managing their new house, and her own general store next to the print shop.

Before long they had two children to help them.

Ben's father made soap and candles for Deborah to sell.

WILLIAM was the oldest.

FRANCIS was born in 1732. When he was four, he got very sick and died.

Baby "SARAH was called "Sally" by her father.

The newspaper was a great success. Then Ben began printing a yearly calendar called Poor Richard's Almanack. The booklet was full of advice, weather forecasts, dates and news. And what made it special were the wise witty sayings of Poor Richard.

Year after year, people bought the almanac. It made Ben famous.

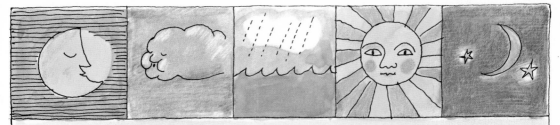

The almanac gave weather forecasts, tide changes, astrology news,

the right time to plant, sow, and harvest,
recipes, cures for ailments, ideas, inventions, news events and

Poor Richard's Sayings:

Early to bed and early to rise, makes a man healthy, wealthy, and wise.

Beware of little expenses. A small leak will sink a great ship.

'Tis hard for an empty bag to stand upright.

Up, sluggard, and waste not life. In the grave will be sleeping enough.

A word to the wise is enough.

At the working man's house, hunger looks in but dares not enter.

Every little makes a mickle.

One today is worth two tomorrows.

Meanwhile, Benjamin Franklin was busy living other lives. He loved Philadelphia. It was a new city full of promise, and Benjamin was there at the right time.

He started a club called the Junto where friends met to discuss books and ideas. It became a school where even today, grownups can go to learn.

Men from many trades came to the Weekly Junto meetings.

He lent out his books. Soon others did the same. This grew into the first free library in America.

He started a fire department, a hospital, a school. He found new ways to light and clean the streets, and helped make laws.

Philadelphia became as famous as Benjamin Franklin.

Benjamin Franklin in his fireman's helmet.

A lamplighter walked through the streets at dusk lighting lamps.

By the time he was 42, Benjamin Franklin had enough money from his printing to live in comfort with his family. He gave up the shop to spend all his time with his ideas. A new life began.

He experimented with electricity. He believed lightning was electricity. He decided to prove it.

During a thunderstorm, he tried a dangerous experiment with a kite and a key, and found he was right.

Now he knew how to protect homes from lightning. He invented lightning rods.

People put "Franklin Rods" up on their rooftops in America and in other countries, too.

Benjamin Franklin's Dangerous Kite Experiment

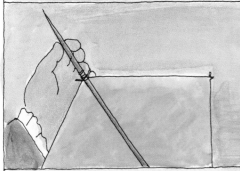

He attached a pointed metal rod to the kite.

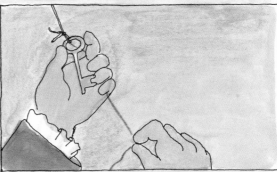

He tied a silk cord to the kite string and a key to the cord.

He and his son, William, took shelter. Lightning struck the rod.

He touched the wet key and felt a shock. Electricity had traveled down the kite string to the key. The silk cord stopped it from going further.

He invented the Franklin Stove in 1744. It fit into a fireplace and could heat a whole house. They are used even today.

He found safer routes for ships to travel.

He became Postmaster General and found safer ways to send mail.

He designed a chair-table.

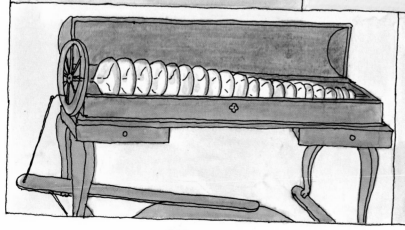

He made a musical instrument called the Armonica in 1762. It was played by rubbing wet fingers against glass discs. Famous composers wrote music for it.

He experimented in his garden and found better ways to grow crops.

He invented glasses called bifocals in 1770. He could see far, out of the top of the glasses, and near, out of the bottom.

He introduced Swiss barley, Chinese rhubarb, Newton apples, willow for baskets, and turnips to America.

He found out that black cloth keeps one warmer than white by laying pieces of cloth in the snow. After some time, the black cloth was warmed by the sun and sank into the snow. The white didn't.

Benjamin Franklin found out many other things in his lifetime. He did not want money for his ideas. He said they belonged to everyone. He wrote them down so that people everywhere could use them. In America and other countries, people took his advice.

Now Benjamin hoped people would listen to his most important idea—freedom for his country. For at that time, America was a colony. He, like others, did not want to be ruled by England any longer.

He was sent to England to seek independence for his country. For 18 years, Benjamin stayed there and worked for that goal.

In 1775 he returned to Philadelphia disappointed. His wife had died. War with England had begun. America was still not free.

Benjamin and his friends discussed ways to gain freedom for America.

He and William left for England. He made many trips back to Philadelphia to visit Deborah and Sally. Deborah did not go with Benjamin because she was afraid of the long dangerous voyage.

Pennsylvania State House, now called Independence Hall, as it looked then.

Benjamin Franklin, Thomas Jefferson, John Adams, John Hancock, and 52 others, signed the Declaration of Independence in Philadelphia on July 4, 1776.

Benjamin Franklin and other great Americans helped Thomas Jefferson write the Declaration of Independence. They were determined that America would be free. But they knew first there would be a long war. And there was.

General George Washington leading a battle during the Revolutionary War.

In France, he visited King Louis XVI and Queen Marie Antoinette.
Though everyone wore fancy clothes and powdered wigs,
Benjamin Franklin did not. Everyone was impressed with
the inventor's plain clothes and simple ways.

He was old and very sick when again Benjamin Franklin sailed away. This time he went to ask the King of France for help.

In France, everyone knew about his inventions and loved him.

Finally the King agreed, and with the aid of France, the war was won. America was free from England at last.

In 1781 the war ended. The Liberty Bell in Independence Hall rang out.

As his ship entered Philadelphia Harbor, bells rang, cannons boomed, and hundreds of people waited to welcome Benjamin Franklin from France.

He was reunited at last with his daughter Sally, her husband Richard Bache, and his grandchildren.

After serving his country abroad, Benjamin Franklin wanted to spend his last years at home. He finally returned from France on September 13, 1785. He thought he had been forgotten.

But he was not forgotten. His country still needed him. He became the first governor of Pennsylvania and helped write the Constitution of the United States.

On September 17, 1787, Benjamin Franklin and the other great writers of the Constitution signed the document on which all laws of the United States are based.

Benjamin Franklin lived 84 years. He left the world his writings, his inventions, his ideas and his wit.

He lived his many lives for us all.